THE *Bill of Rights*

Our Government and Citizenship

SPIRIT of America®

THE *Bill of Rights*

By Michael Teitelbaum

Content Adviser: David R. Smith, PhD, Academic Advisor and Adjunct Assistant Professor of History, The University of Michigan, Ann Arbor, Michigan

The Child's World
The Child's World
Chanhassen, Minnesota

THE *Bill of Rights*

Published in the United States of America by The Child's World®
PO Box 326 • Chanhassen, MN 55317-0326 • 800-599-READ • www.childsworld.com

Acknowledgments
　The Child's World®: Mary Berendes, Publishing Director

　Editorial Directions, Inc.: E. Russell Primm, Editorial Director; Pam Rosenberg, Line Editor; Katie Marsico, Associate Editor; Judi Shiffer, Associate Editor and Library Media Specialist; Matthew Messbarger, Editorial Assistant; Susan Hindman, Copy Editor; Lucia Raatma, Proofreader; Judith Frisbee, Peter Garnham, and Olivia Nellums, Fact Checkers; Tim Griffin/IndexServ, Indexer; Cian Loughlin O'Day, Photo Researcher; Linda S. Koutris, Photo Selector

Photo
　Cover: Cover/frontispiece: Comstock/Punchstock.
　Interior: AP/Wide World/Akira Ono: 13; Bettmann/Corbis: 7, 8, 9, 19, 20, 21, 23, 26; Corbis: 11 (Burstein Collection), 14 (Dale C. Spartas), 15, 16, 17 (Robert Essel NYC), 18 (Joseph Sohm; ChromoSohm Inc.), 22 (Matthew Mendelsohn), 28 (Kevin Fleming); Getty Images: 12 (Time Life Pictures/Steve Liss), 25 (Photodisc/Doug Menuez); Getty Images/Hulton|Archive: 6, 10.

Registration
　The Child's World®, Spirit of America®, and their associated logos are the sole property and registered trademarks of The Child's World®.

　Copyright ©2005 by The Child's World®. All rights reserved. No part of this book may be reproduced or utilized in any form or by any means without written permission from the publisher.

Library of Congress Cataloging-in-Publication Data
　Teitelbaum, Michael.
　　The Bill of Rights / by Michael Teitelbaum.
　　　p. cm. — (Our government and citizenship)
　　Includes bibliographical references (p.　) and index.
　　ISBN 1-59296-328-5 (lib. bdg. : alk. paper) 1. United States. Constitution. 1st-10th Amendments—Juvenile literature. I. Title. II. Series.
　　KF4750.T448 2004
　　342.7308'5—dc22　　　　　　　　　　　　2004006043

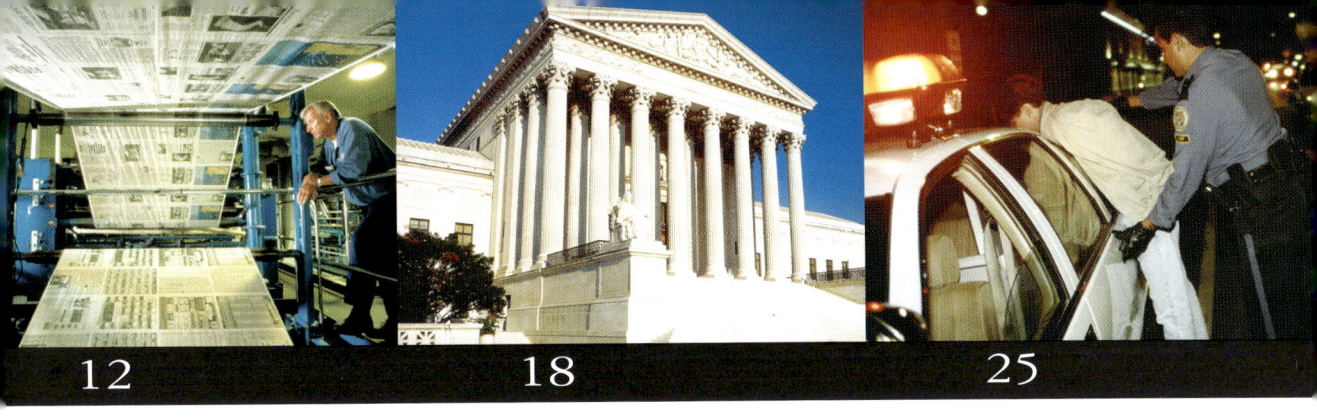

Contents

Chapter ONE	Why a Bill of Rights?		6
Chapter TWO	The First 10 Amendments		12
Chapter THREE	The Bill of Rights in Action—Famous Cases		18
Chapter FOUR	More Famous Cases		24
	Time Line		29
	Glossary Terms		30
	For Further Information		31
	Index		32

Chapter ONE

Why a Bill of Rights?

THE YEAR WAS 1783. THE AMERICAN REVOLUTION was finally over, after eight bloody years of conflict. The 13 American colonies had banded together to defeat the British. With the costly war behind them, they now had the difficult task of deciding what kind of government the young country wanted.

New York burns during the British occupation of the city in 1776.

Independence Hall in Philadelphia, Pennsylvania, was the site of the Constitutional Convention of 1787.

At the time, a document called the Articles of Confederation established certain rules that bound the 13 individual colonies together into a union. But this document was not perfect. It did not provide for many things the new nation needed, such as a way to gather money to pay off debts and a way to raise an army in case of war.

In May 1787, 55 **delegates** from the 13 American colonies—which now called themselves states—met in Philadelphia. These delegates knew they needed a stronger document upon which to base their new country. The document they wrote over the next four months became the Constitution of the United States.

Interesting Fact

▸ In September 1787, the Constitution was completed and signed by 39 of the 55 delegates to the Constitutional Convention. The delegates agreed that it would take effect when 9 of the original 13 colonies approved the document. Delaware was the first state to approve the Constitution in December 1787. New Hampshire was the ninth state to approve the document on June 21, 1788. On that day, the U.S. Constitution took effect and the United States of America became a nation.

George Mason was born in Fairfax County, Virginia, in 1725. Though he was a southerner, he strongly opposed slavery and was against allowing the slave trade to continue under the new constitution.

The new Constitution spelled out how the government would be set up. It also transferred a great deal of power from the individual states to the new federal government. Instead of each state doing things its own way, the United States of America now had a unified set of rules for all states to follow. Still, many at this Constitutional Convention felt that something was missing. After years of heavy-handed rule by the British king and Parliament, a number of the delegates were worried. They feared that this new Constitution, which gave so much power to the centralized federal government, would not protect the rights of individual Americans.

As great a document as it was, the Constitution did not guarantee the American people individual rights such as freedom of speech, freedom of the press, and freedom to practice the religion of their choice. Delegates such as Edmund Randolph and George Mason, both of Virginia, spoke strongly of the need for a bill of rights to be part of the Constitution. They wanted the people of the United States to be guaranteed these freedoms.

Models for the Bill of Rights

THROUGHOUT HISTORY, THERE HAVE BEEN OTHER DOCUMENTS WRITTEN that attempted to guarantee people certain rights. In England in 1215, the Magna Carta (being signed by King John, below) first put forward the concept of a trial by a jury of peers and a fair court system. In 1628, the British Parliament passed the Petition of Rights, which prevented the king from forcing people to house troops in their homes. In 1689, the British Parliament adopted the English Bill of Rights, which stated that no king could control Parliament and that members of Parliament could not be punished for disagreeing with the king. The Declaration of Independence, adopted by the American colonists in 1776, states that all men have certain rights, such as life, liberty, and the pursuit of happiness.

9

Thomas Jefferson was born in Shadwell, Virginia, in 1743. He was the main author of the Declaration of Independence.

Despite the protest of these delegates, the Constitution was passed in June 1788 without a bill of rights attached. It became the foundation for running the American government and has remained in effect for more than 200 years.

Over the next few years, leaders of the young nation continued to push for a bill of rights to be added to the Constitution. Thomas Jefferson of Virginia, who would go on to become the third president of the United States, wrote to his friend James Madison. Madison, a fellow Virginian, had been one of the leaders of the Constitutional Convention.

Jefferson wrote that ". . . a bill of rights, providing clearly for freedom of religion, freedom of the press, and trials by jury, is what the people are entitled to against every government on earth . . . and what no just government should refuse."

Madison, who had not been a strong supporter of a bill of rights during the convention, eventually came around

James Madison was born in Port Conway, Virginia, in 1751. A believer in the need for a strong central government, he wrote The Federalist *with Alexander Hamilton and John Jay.*

to his friend's way of thinking. Madison, along with a few other like-minded members of Congress, drafted a set of 12 **amendments.** If passed by the states, these amendments would be added to the end of the Constitution.

On December 15, 1791, three years after the Constitution was ratified, 10 of the 12 amendments were approved by the states. They became the first 10 amendments to be added as a permanent part of the Constitution and are known as the Bill of Rights.

Interesting Fact

▶ In 1941, President Franklin D. Roosevelt signed a bill proclaiming December 15 as Bill of Rights Day. It was on this date in 1791 that the Bill of Rights was adopted by the states and made part of the U.S. Constitution.

11

Chapter **Two**

The First 10 Amendments

THE BILL OF RIGHTS FORMS THE BASIS FOR THE freedoms that citizens of the United States still enjoy. But what are these rights, and how do they apply to Americans today?

The First Amendment guarantees freedom of religion, speech, and the press. The government

A newspaper is printed under the watchful eye of a worker. The freedom to print whatever a publisher wishes to print—even criticism of the president or other government officials—in the newspaper is guaranteed by the First Amendment.

A synagogue, or Jewish house of worship, in New York. Citizens of the United States are free to practice any religion they choose.

cannot interfere with these rights. It also guarantees the right of people to assemble peacefully and to **petition** the government for changes.

Americans can practice any religion they choose or none at all. They can say what they like, as long as they are not putting anyone else in danger. People in the United States are also free to gather in groups to protest the policies of their government and to petition their government to change those policies.

The Second Amendment guarantees the right to bear arms. This means that the federal government

Interesting Fact

▶ In the 1970s, large protests helped bring an end to the Vietnam War (1957–1975). More recently, in 2003, antiwar protestors gathered in cities around the United States to express their opposition to the war in Iraq.

This duck hunter, like all Americans, is free to own a gun. This right is guaranteed by the Second Amendment.

cannot pass laws preventing people from owning guns. This amendment was written to keep state **militias** well armed against foreign invasion. Today, some people believe that, because there are no longer state militias, this amendment does not give private citizens the right to own guns. Others believe that the amendment gives them the right to own guns for recreation and for defending their homes, businesses, and families.

The Third Amendment prevents the government from housing soldiers in private homes, something the British did during the colonial years. This almost never occurs anymore.

The Fourth Amendment protects people from unreasonable search and seizure. Search **warrants** must be obtained from a judge before someone's home, belongings, or person can be searched. Today, before a judge will issue a warrant, police must convince the judge that the search of a specific location will help them find evidence of a crime.

The Fifth Amendment establishes the rights of a person accused of a crime. Today, during a trial, a person may say, "I refuse to answer that question on the grounds that it may **incriminate** me." People cannot be forced to testify against themselves. Also, no one can be tried twice for the same crime. The Fifth Amendment also states that the government cannot take a person's private property for public use without giving that person fair compensation.

The Sixth Amendment guarantees a person accused of a crime the right to a speedy and public trial by an **impartial** jury, and the right to a lawyer for his or her defense. This amendment prevents

A witness is sworn in at a trial. Citizens called to testify at a trial are sworn to tell the truth. But, thanks to the Fifth Amendment, a citizen accused of a crime has the right to refuse to answer a question if he believes the answer will cause him to be found guilty of the crime.

When court is in session, a jury may sit in the jury box on the left side of this courtroom. The Sixth Amendment guarantees that a person accused of a crime will get a trial in front of an impartial jury.

people from being kept in jail for years without the right to defend themselves. Today, law enforcement officers must inform people being arrested that they have these rights.

The Seventh Amendment gives people the right to a jury trial in a federal civil suit. This is a suit involving a claim of damage in which money is sought. For example, if two people from different states have a car accident, they have the right to a federal trial to sort out the damages.

The Eighth Amendment prohibits cruel and unusual punishment. In colonial times, torture was sometimes used against those who had been arrested. Today, a person is considered innocent until he or she is found guilty in a trial, and torture is not allowed, no matter how serious the crime. It also prevents a judge from requiring that unreasonable bail or fines be paid. Bail is money that must be paid for a person to get out of jail while waiting for the trial to begin.

The Ninth Amendment says that people have certain basic human rights. Even though a certain right is not specifically mentioned in the Constitution or the Bill of Rights, that doesn't mean that people don't have this right.

The Tenth Amendment states that the federal government has only the powers outlined in the Constitution. All other powers, except those specifically denied to the states, are reserved for the states. Today, for example, states make their own decisions about how to run their schools because this power was not given to the federal government by the Constitution.

A police officer arrests a suspected criminal. When a police officer arrests someone, that person must be informed of his or her rights under the Fifth Amendment. These rights are often called Miranda Rights after the famous Supreme Court case Miranda v. Arizona.

Chapter THREE

The Bill of Rights in Action—Famous Cases

IN THE YEARS SINCE THE BILL OF RIGHTS WAS ADDED to the U.S. Constitution, many court cases have used these 10 amendments as the basis for their arguments. Most of these cases were heard by the U.S. Supreme Court. Here are some examples.

As African-Americans fought for civil rights in the 1960s, the courts often had to decide if large

The U.S. Supreme Court Building in Washington, D.C., was completed in 1935. Before that time, the Supreme Court did not have a building of its own.

Civil rights protestors march on Washington, D.C., in 1963.

protest gatherings on public property were protected by the First Amendment. On March 2, 1961, 187 African-American high school and college students in Columbia, South Carolina, held a demonstration to protest racial **discrimination.** When the police ordered them to leave, they refused and were then arrested. In the case called *Edwards v. South Carolina,* the Supreme Court ruled in favor of the demonstrators, stating that they were protected by their rights to free speech, free assembly, and freedom to petition the government for change.

For many years, prayer in public school was not required by law but was a common practice. In the early 1960s, New York State officials began requiring all students to say a prayer aloud in their classrooms at the start of the school day. The

Interesting Fact

▸ The march on Washington, D.C., took place on August 28, 1963. A crowd of more than 200,000 people gathered near the Lincoln Memorial to demand equal rights for all citizens. It was at this gathering that Martin Luther King Jr. delivered his famous "I Have a Dream" speech.

Texas students pray in their classroom. In Engel v. Vitale, *the Supreme Court said that students could not be required to pray in school.*

parents of 10 students sued the state, claiming that this policy violated the First Amendment, which states that no law can be made establishing religion. They said it also violated the idea of the separation of church and state, set forth by the Constitution. In 1962, in the case called *Engel v. Vitale,* the court ruled in favor of the parents, saying that mandatory school prayer violated the First Amendment. It said that the government had no business composing "official prayers for any group of the American people."

In 1965, several students in Des Moines, Iowa, wore black armbands to school to protest U.S. involvement in the Vietnam War. Mary Beth Tinker, her brother John Tinker, and their friend

Christopher Eckhardt were all suspended for violating the school's dress code. The Tinkers' father sued the school system. The case, called *Tinker v. Des Moines Independent Community School District,* reached the Supreme Court in 1969. The Supreme Court ruled in favor of the students, stating that the wearing of armbands in protest was a legitimate form of symbolic speech and was therefore protected by the First Amendment.

In 1984, Gregory Johnson burned an American flag outside the Republican National Convention in Dallas, Texas. Johnson said that this was an act of protest against the policies of President Ronald Reagan. Texas officials charged Johnson with violating a state law prohibiting the destruction of an American flag. In the case called *Texas v. Johnson,* the Supreme Court ruled that the state could not convict Johnson and that the state law was not consistent with the

Gregory Johnson holds the flag he burned in protest of American policies under President Ronald Reagan. The Supreme Court upheld his right to burn the flag as a protest, saying that it was a form of free speech.

Janet Reno became the first female Attorney General of the United States in 1993. The 1997 Supreme Court case, Reno v. ACLU, *bears her name.*

First Amendment. The court ruled that the act of burning the flag was a form of expression similar to the free speech guaranteed by the First Amendment.

Although radio, television, and the Internet did not exist when the Bill of Rights was written, the principles of the great document can be applied to our changing world. In 1996, Congress passed a law called the Communications Decency Act, designed to protect children from "offensive" and "indecent" speech online. The American Civil Liberties Union (ACLU) and other groups challenged this law. They felt that it would infringe on the free speech rights of adults using the Internet. In 1997, in a case called *Reno v. ACLU,* the Supreme Court ruled in favor of the ACLU. The Court stated that the Internet deserved the highest degree of protection under the First Amendment.

Civil Liberties

DURING TIMES OF WAR, THE GOVERNMENT HAS SOMETIMES RESTRICTED the civil liberties guaranteed to citizens by the Bill of Rights. During World War II (1939–1945), Japanese Americans were rounded up and placed in prison camps on the orders of President Franklin Roosevelt. One of his generals, John L. De Witt, justified this action, saying: "They are a dangerous element. There is no way to determine their loyalty. It makes no difference if an **internee** is an American. Theoretically he is still Japanese, and you can't change him by giving him a piece of paper."

But after the government searched the homes of many internees, Francis Biddle (below), the attorney general at that time, said: "We have not uncovered through these searches any dangerous persons that we could not otherwise know about. We have not found any evidence of any bombs or guns. We have not found a camera which we have reason to believe was used in espionage."

The debate over whether the civil liberties of these Japanese Americans were violated continues to this day.

23

Chapter Four

More Famous Cases

Interesting Fact

▸ The National Rifle Association was founded in 1871 by Colonel William C. Church and General George Wingate. Both men fought for the Union during the Civil War and had been unhappy with the poor marksmanship skills of their troops. Ambrose Burnside, a Civil War general, U.S. Senator, and former governor of Rhode Island, became the first president of the organization.

In 1981, the Chicago suburb of Morton Grove, Illinois, became the first town in the United States to ban the possession of handguns by private citizens. Only police, military personnel, prison officials, and licensed gun collectors could own guns. The National Rifle Association (NRA), a group that represents gun owners, took the town to court. The Supreme Court refused to hear the case, which was called *Quilici v. the Village of Morton Grove.* A lower court ruling stood, which said that the city law had not violated the Second Amendment. That court ruled that "possession of handguns by individuals is not part of the right to bear arms." They stated that local and state governments were allowed to pass gun laws, and that the Second Amendment applied to militias, not individuals.

In 1982, during a statewide strike of prison guards in New York, the prison removed several of the striking guards from their homes at the prison facility. The state then placed National Guard troops in those residences.

Two of the displaced guards sued the prison, claiming that their Third Amendment rights had been violated. They compared the housing of National Guard troops in their homes to the housing of British troops in the homes of colonists. A federal appeals court ruled that the Third Amendment did protect the guards and guaranteed them a "legitimate expectation of privacy."

In 2000, the Supreme Court heard the case of *Florida v. J. L.,* in which a juvenile was accused of illegally possessing a gun. In this case, an anonymous person called the police to tell them that a young man in a plaid shirt was standing at a bus stop carrying a gun. The police went to the bus stop and found the man who did have a gun. But the Court threw out the case, as a violation of the Fourth Amendment, saying that the police did not have enough reasonable suspi-

A police officer frisks a suspect to be sure he doesn't have a weapon that can be used against the officer. Whether or not regular citizens should be allowed to carry guns is a question that is still being debated today.

Ernesto Miranda (right) speaks with his attorney. The Supreme Court overturned Miranda's conviction when it was proven that he had not been informed of his right to remain silent and to have an attorney present during questioning.

cion to search the man. A search cannot be allowed based on what they called "a bare report of an unknown, unaccountable informant."

The following year, the Supreme Court ruled that Indianapolis police officers violated the Fourth Amendment by randomly stopping people to determine if they were carrying illegal drugs. They stated that the officers could not have had "probable cause," the belief that an individual is breaking the law, for every single person who had been randomly stopped.

In 1963, a man named Ernesto Miranda was arrested on charges of kidnapping and raping an 18-

year-old girl in Phoenix, Arizona. Miranda signed a confession following two hours of intense police questioning. The police, however, did not inform Miranda that he had the right to remain silent, the right to have an attorney present during questioning, and the right to not incriminate, or put the blame, on himself. Miranda received a sentence of 20 to 30 years in jail. Then, in 1966, his lawyers appealed. The case, *Miranda v. Arizona* went to the Supreme Court, which ruled that the arresting police officers violated the Fifth Amendment by not informing Miranda of his rights. Miranda was released from prison. Today, when police officers inform people being arrested of their Fifth Amendments rights, the officers are said to be reading them their "Miranda rights."

In 1992, the Supreme Court ruled in the case called *Doggett v. United States,* that a defendant's Sixth Amendment right to a speedy trial was violated. That defendant had been forced to wait eight and a half years from the time he was arrested to the time of his trial.

The Eighth Amendment prohibits cruel and unusual punishment. For years, the most controversial cases relating to this amendment came from the legal debate as to whether or not the death penalty is cruel and unusual punishment. In three different cases in 1972, the Supreme Court ruled that all death penalty laws violated the Eighth Amendment. These rulings ended the use of the death penalty in the United States at that time. Then in 1976, in the case called *Gregg v.*

Interesting Fact

▸ Ernesto Miranda died in 1976 after being stabbed in a fight. Police arrested a suspect who exercised his Fifth Amendment rights to remain silent and was released.

Georgia, the Supreme Court ruled that punishment by death for the crime of murder does not violate the Eighth Amendment. Today, states are free to adopt their own laws regarding the death penalty.

In the 1973 case called *Roe v. Wade,* the Supreme Court upheld a woman's right to choose whether or not to end a pregnancy. It also upheld the right of a doctor to treat a patient according to that doctor's best medical judgment. These rights are not specifically mentioned in the Constitution. The court based its decision on the power of the Ninth Amendment to guarantee rights not listed in the Constitution.

In the 1995 case called *United States v. Lopez,* the Supreme Court ruled that the 1990 federal law creating gun-free zones near schools violated the Tenth Amendment. The Court stated that Congress did not have the right to pass a law that dealt with an issue of state and local concern. According to the Tenth Amendment, any power not given to the federal government by the Constitution automatically belongs to the states.

As these cases show, the brilliance of the Bill of Rights is that it is a living, **flexible** document. Although it was written more than 200 years ago, it still applies to life in the United States today.

The Bill of Rights memorialized on a bronze plaque.

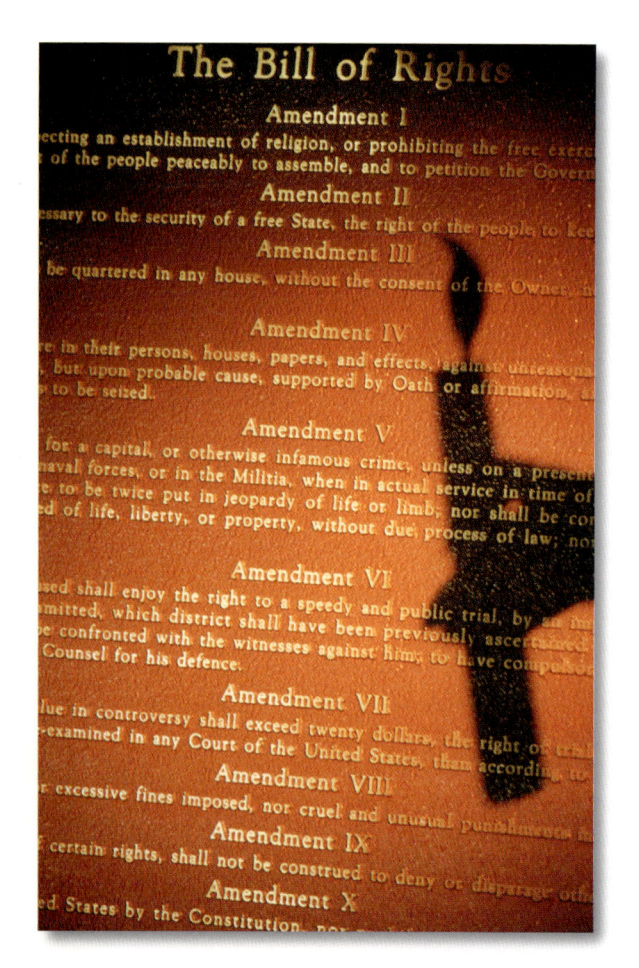

Time LINE

1776   1803   1984

1776 The Declaration of Independence is adopted by the American colonists.

1781 The Articles of Confederation are ratified; they establish certain rules that bind the 13 individual colonies together as a union.

1783 The Revolutionary War ends.

1787 On September 17, the Constitutional Convention approves the Constitution.

1788 The U.S. Constitution takes effect when New Hampshire approves it on June 21.

1789 The Supreme Court is created by the Constitution on September 24.

1791 On December 15, the Bill of Rights is approved by the states.

1803 The Supreme Court acts against Congress in *Marbury v. Madison* and establishes the Court's power to strike down any act of Congress that violates the Constitution.

1920 The American Civil Liberties Union (ACLU) is formed and dedicates itself to holding the government to the Bill of Rights' promises.

1961 *Edwards v. South Carolina* goes to the Supreme Court; the Court rules that demonstrators are protected by the First Amendment.

1962 *Engel v. Vitale* goes to the Supreme Court; the Court rules that school prayer violates the First Amendment.

1966 The Miranda rights are established in the *Miranda v. Arizona* case.

1969 The *Tinker v. Des Moines Independent Community School District* case goes to the Supreme Court.

1981 The *Quilici v. the Village of Morton Grove* case is refused a hearing by the Supreme Court.

1984 The Supreme Court case *Texas v. Johnson* declares that the burning of the flag is a form of expression similar to free speech.

1997 *Reno v. ACLU,* a Supreme Court case, protects the Internet under the First Amendment.

2000 In *Florida v. J. L.,* the Supreme Court rules that police do not have the right to search without reasonable suspicion.

29

Glossary Terms

amendments (uh-MEND-muhnts)
Amendments are changes made to laws or documents. The first 10 amendments to the Constitution are known as the Bill of Rights.

delegates (DEL-uh-guhts)
Delegates are representatives or spokespersons. Fifty-five delegates from the 13 American colonies met in Philadelphia in May 1787.

discrimination (diss-krim-i-NAY-shuhn)
Discrimination is the act of showing prejudice or intolerance based on differences in age, race, gender, religion, or other personal characteristics. On March 2, 1961, 187 African-American high school and college students in Columbia, South Carolina, held a demonstration to protest racial discrimination.

flexible (FLEK-suh-buhl)
Something that is flexible can be adapted to new, changing circumstances. The Bill of Rights is a living, flexible document.

impartial (im-PAHR-shuhl)
To be impartial is to be fair and not favor one person or point of view over another. The Sixth Amendment guarantees a person accused of a crime the right to a fair and speedy trial by an impartial jury.

incriminate (in-KRIM-uh-nate)
To incriminate means to put the blame on. People cannot be forced to incriminate themselves.

internee (in-turn-EE)
An internee is someone held in a prison. One of President Roosevelt's generals said, "It makes no difference if an internee is an American."

militias (muh-LISH-uhz)
Militias are armed forces made up of ordinary citizens prepared to fight in case of an emergency. The Second Amendment was written to keep state militias well armed against foreign invasion.

petition (peh-TIH-shuhn)
To petition someone is to ask them—often through the use of a formal, written document—to do something. The First Amendment guarantees citizens the right to petition the government for changes.

warrants (WOR-uhnts)
Warrants are documents, signed by a judge, that allow police to search for evidence of a crime. Arrest warrants must be obtained from a judge before someone's home, belongings, or person can be searched.

For Further Information

On the Web

Visit our home page for lots of links about the Bill of Rights:
http://www.childsworld.com/links.html

Note to Parents, Teachers, and Librarians:
We routinely verify our Web links to make sure they're safe, active sites—so encourage your readers to check them out!

Books

Hudson Jr., David L. *The Bill of Rights.* Berkeley Heights, N.J.: Enslow Publishers, Inc., 2002.

Krull, Kathleen, and Anna Divito (illustrator). *A Kids' Guide to America's Bill of Rights: Curfews, Censorship, and the 100-Pound Giant.* New York: Avon, 1999.

Nardo, Don. *The Bill of Rights.* San Diego, Calif.: Greenhaven Press, Inc., 1998.

Places to Visit or Contact

Independence National Historical Park
To visit Independence Hall and learn more about the Constitution of the United States
143 South Third Street
Philadelphia, PA 19106
215/597-8974

The National Archives Experience
To see the original Constitution and Bill of Rights documents and learn more about them
700 Pennsylvania Avenue NW
Washington, DC 20408
866/272-6272

Index

American Civil Liberties Union (ACLU), 22
American Revolution, 6
Articles of Confederation, 7

Bill of Rights Day, 11

civil rights, 18
Communications Decency Act, 22
Constitution of the United States, 7–8, 10, 11, 17, 20, 28
Constitutional Convention, 8

De Witt, John L., 23
death penalty, 27–28
Declaration of Independence, 9
delegates, 7, 8, 10
discrimination, 19
Doggett v. United States, 27

Eckhardt, Christopher, 21
Edwards v. South Carolina, 19
Eighth Amendment, 16–17, 27–28
Engel v. Vitale, 20
English Bill of Rights, 9

Fifth Amendment, 15, 27
First Amendment, 12–13, 19, 20, 21, 22
Florida v. J. L., 25
Fourth Amendment, 14, 25–26

Great Britain, 6, 9
Gregg v. Georgia, 27–28

Internet, 22

Japanese Americans, 23
Jefferson, Thomas, 10
Johnson, Gregory, 21–22

Madison, James, 10–11
Magna Carta, 9
Mason, George, 8
Miranda, Ernesto, 26–27
Miranda rights, 27
Miranda v. Arizona, 27

National Rifle Association (NRA), 24
Ninth Amendment, 17, 28

Parliament, 9
Petition of Rights, 9
probable cause, 26

Quilici v. the Village of Morton Grove, 24

Randolph, Edmund, 8
ratification, 11
Reno v. ACLU, 22
Roe v. Wade, 28
Roosevelt, Franklin Delano, 11, 23

school prayer, 19–20
Second Amendment, 13–14, 24
separation of church and state, 20
Seventh Amendment, 16
Sixth Amendment, 15–16, 27
state militias, 14, 24
states, 7, 11, 28

Tenth Amendment, 17, 28
Texas v. Johnson, 21–22
Third Amendment, 14, 25
Tinker, John, 20–21
Tinker, Mary Beth, 20–21
Tinker v. Des Moines Independent Community School District, 21

United States v. Lopez, 28

Vietnam War, 13, 20

warrants, 14
World War II, 23

About the Author

MICHAEL TEITELBAUM HAS BEEN A WRITER AND EDITOR OF children's books and magazines for more than 20 years. In addition to his nonfiction writing, Michael has also written many books based on popular cartoon characters such as Garfield and Superman. He recently wrote a novel based on the television show *Smallville,* and three novels based on the television show *Justice League.* Michael and his wife, Sheleigah, split their time between New York City and their 160-year-old farmhouse in the Catskill Mountains of upstate New York.

HLOOX + 342 .73 T

TEITELBAUM, MICHAEL.
THE BILL OF RIGHTS

LOOSCAN
05/07